Original title:
The Sweet Scent of Gingerbread

Copyright © 2024 Creative Arts Management OÜ
All rights reserved.

Author: Milo Harrington
ISBN HARDBACK: 978-9916-90-860-0
ISBN PAPERBACK: 978-9916-90-861-7

Sugar-Coated Reminiscences

In a kitchen of chaos, flour flies about,
Ginger men wrestle, there's laughter and shout.
A rolling pin dances, who needs a partner?
The dog snatches crumbs, he's a true charmer.

Sugar sprinkles like confetti in air,
Baking soda makes explosions, we can't help but stare.
The timer rings loud, but we're still in a trance,
As marshmallow fluff joins in for the dance.

The taste of the batter, oh, such a delight,
A spoonful for me, then I'll give it a bite.
But wait, there's a whisk stuck right in my hair,
I laugh till I cry; it's a messy affair.

Rolling out dough, it just won't behave,
It sticks to the counter as I dig like a slave.
But the smell fills the room and it piques my delight,
As we toss all our worries and frolic through the night.

Molasses Moonlight

Under the starry glaze, they mix it right,
Rolling dough in the soft moonlight.
Flour fights dance, a sugary spree,
Giggles and crumbs, as sweet as can be.

The oven's a dragon, it roars with heat,
While cookies hide, their flavor's a treat.
Dancing around with giddy delight,
They race to the table, what a sight!

Frosting Dreams and Ginger Schemes

Whisking and swirling, oh what a fun,
Splattering frosting, we've just begun!
Chefs in aprons, a colorful crew,
Taste-testing ginger, just to get through.

Piping in patterns, a cake in the round,
Rainbows of colors all over the ground.
Laughter erupts as sprinkles take flight,
Gingerbread houses stand tall with delight!

Baked with Love

In the cozy kitchen, a jolly affair,
Measuring sugar with utmost care.
But flour exploits, it flies through the air,
Good luck smearing it in my hair!

Rolling and shaping, oh what a mess,
Gingerbread men in their festive dress.
Some have no buttons, just smiles at best,
Who knew this chaos could be such a fest?

A Symphony of Spices

Cardamom and cinnamon make their great debut,
Singing through the kitchen, oh what a view!
Nutmeg's a soloist, bold and spry,
While the ginger plays along, watch it fly!

They harmonize sweetly in batter so fine,
Mixing together, oh what a design!
A chorus of flavors, a jazzy delight,
Time to bake cookies, let's party all night!

Candied Comforts

In the kitchen, chaos reigns,
Flour flying like ghostly trains.
Sugar spills like whispered dreams,
Laughter's sweet, or so it seems.

Baking cookies, oh what a feat,
Burnt edges, can't take the heat!
Ginger snaps dance on the floor,
Someone's trying to fix the door!

Hearthside Delights

The oven hums a jolly tune,
While I hop like a Christmas goon.
Rolling dough with sugar glee,
I've made a mess—oh dear me!

Eggs go flying, what a show!
My apron's lost; it's in the dough.
Frosting fights and icing wars,
Who knew baking could cause such wars?

The Enchanted Oven

In a magical realm of spice,
The cookies bake and all is nice.
But wait! What's that? A puff of smoke?
My treats might just be a cruel joke!

With a wink and a sprinkle of cheer,
Each batch may vanish, oh dear, oh dear!
But with giggles rising like the bread,
Each silly failure is more fun instead!

Winter's Sugary Embrace

Snowflakes dance outside the glass,
While inside, dough begins to amass.
With ginger and giggles round the bowl,
I'm not sure who's more out of control!

Piping icing with a shaky hand,
I turn my creation to a gingerbread band.
Candied buttons, on looks I'm a wreck,
It's a sugary wonder, what the heck!

Fragrant Trails of Cinnamon

In the kitchen, chaos reigns,
Flour flies like snowy grains.
Ginger folks dance on the floor,
While cookies giggle, beg for more.

A whisk took flight, oh what a sight,
The dog was covered, a furry white.
We chased him round, a merry chase,
While laughter filled the crowded space.

Baked Wonders in a Frosty Landscape

Out in the cold, I brave the frost,
My mittened hands, oh how they are lost!
Heavenly scents waft through the air,
As I nibble a treat, without a care.

The snowmen nearby, they start to grin,
With cookie buttons and a chocolate chin.
They laugh at my clumsiness, what a show,
As I topple over from too much dough.

Sweetening Winter's Chill

Snowflakes twirl like sprightly sprites,
As ginger shapes take fluffy flights.
Hot cocoa spills—a delightful mess,
On a couch that's seen much better dress.

The cat, bemused, licks her paws,
While my brother claims the last of the raws.
We giggle as he makes a face,
Spices tumbling, a kooky race.

Savoring the Hearth's Embrace

Toasty warmth around us glows,
Where the whiff of sweetness flows.
A ginger man dreams of escape,
While we plan his frosting drape.

Friends unite with sprinkles bright,
In a battle of icing, what a sight!
Laughter erupts in cookie wars,
As crumbs and giggles spread on floors.

Sugar-Rimmed Memories

In the kitchen, chaos reigns,
Flour flies like dancing grains.
Spilled sugar, oh what a mess,
Tasted and laughed, more or less.

Frosting fights with candy canes,
Who knew sweets could cause such pains?
Baking dreams take flight in jest,
With crumbs that dress the very best.

A Dusting of Winter Cheer

Snowflakes fall on sugar hills,
Baking brings its quirky thrills.
Piper the cat sneaks a taste,
Mischief makes the joy go fast.

Laughter echoes, pots a-clatter,
While tinsel gleams and dreams scatter.
Rolling dough with goofy flair,
Gingerbread men dance unaware.

Sweet Serenades from the Oven

The oven hums a cheery tune,
Cookies dance like a cartoon.
Whisking up a melody,
Sugar-coated harmony!

Silly hats on ginger folks,
Peppermint sticks and funny jokes.
Laughter wafts, the scent's divine,
All chaos, but oh so fine!

Frost-kissed Cookie Kaleidoscope

Colors bright as candy dreams,
In this kitchen, nothing's as seems.
Gingerbread in funny poses,
Dressed with joy, like silly roses.

Chasing crumbs like little mice,
Can't decide which one looks nice.
In every bite, a giggle's found,
Laughing with each sugary round.

Joyous Fragments of Frostedness

Frosting flung like a snowball's flight,
Ginger men dance in the pale moonlight.
Sprinkles scatter, oh what a sight,
Laughter erupts, what pure delight!

Cookies collide, a sugary mess,
Who knew baking could cause such stress?
The dough fights back, a fluffy press,
Each bite brings flavor, we feel so blessed.

Sweetness from the Oven

The oven hums a cheerful tune,
While flour flies like a little monsoon.
Batter spills, oh my! What a boon,
Crazy chaos would make a raccoon swoon.

A pinch of this and a dash of that,
Cookie thieves, imagine the spat!
Gingerbread cookies thrown, what a chat,
We munch on crumbs till we fall flat!

Fragrant Tales of a Winter Bake

Whisking wildly with giggles galore,
A dash too much, what's one more?
The cat's on the counter, chasing some more,
We'll blame the sugar high for the uproar!

Sticky fingers, sweet frosting fights,
As we craft creatures with silly sights.
Gingerbread warriors in epic nights,
They battle sprinkles, oh what delights!

Warm Spice, Warm Hearts

From the warmth of the oven, a whiff does soar,
Chasing sweet dreams, forever in store.
Each cookie a hug that we can't ignore,
Let's bake our troubles, who could want more?

Baking blunders that bring silly rhyme,
Our floury friends laughing in time.
Silly shapes like a twisted climb,
But oh, the taste! It's simply sublime!

Cookies Beneath the Stars

Under twinkling lights, we bake,
With sugar high and laughter's ache.
A sprinkle here, a sprinkle there,
The flour flies like we don't care.

The oven hums a merry tune,
As we dance around, a silly boon.
Brownie points for every flub,
Our kitchen's now a laughter hub.

Scented Stories of Yule

Once a cookie tried to flee,
Oh, how it rolled—it tripped on me!
The frosting swirled, a ghastly sight,
It looked like frosting had taken flight.

With every batch, a tale unfolds,
A cookie thief with dreams so bold.
While giggles bubble like hot soup,
The dough grows legs to join our troop.

Ginger's Golden Glow

Ginger leaps and bounds away,
Sweet spice giving kids a play.
Rooftop acrobat in the night,
Baking dreams with pure delight.

The dough's too soft; it starts to flop,
They land a jump, a sugar plop.
Golden hues and snickers, too,
As we munch on the failed brew.

Warmth in Every Bite

A cookie smiles with chocolate eyes,
In our smiles, it finds its prize.
With belly laughs, we munch away,
'Till crumbs unite in a bouncy play.

The warmth escapes, like giggles free,
As we feast on this crispy spree.
With every crunch, a bit of cheer,
Our funny feast, the best time of year.

Whispers of Cinnamon Dreams

In the kitchen, chaos reigns,
Flour flies like tiny planes.
The mixer's dancing, oh what joy,
As sugar lands like a playful toy.

Nuts and fruits begin to blend,
I swear they have a will to bend.
Spices giggle, take a chance,
While dough does a lively dance.

Rolling, pinching, what a mess,
The cat's now donned a chef's dress.
With every scoop, the laughter grows,
Who knew baking could be such a show?

Finally baked, oh what a sight,
Gingerbread men running with delight.
But hold your horses, take a seat,
The icing's wild — a sugar treat!

A Warm Hearth's Embrace

With every crackle, warmth does spread,
A cinnamon spell weaves in our head.
The pumpkin's dressed in a funny hat,
The oven's hum sounds just like a cat.

Twinkle lights are hanging here,
While gingerbread folks lend their cheer.
They wobble, giggle, take a stroll,
With frosting rivers, they lose control.

A sprinkle here, a dash of flair,
The sugar high is beyond compare.
Adulting's tough, but here we play,
With every bite, we drift away.

Wrapped in laughter, sweet delight,
The hearth's embrace feels just right.
So grab a cookie, take a friend,
This sugary tale will never end!

Sugar-Spiced Memories

A whisk in hand, what could go wrong?
Mixing sweet tunes in a silly song.
The measuring cups held like a mic,
As flour puffs like a frosty bike.

Giggles echo as dough is tossed,
But oh dear, what a festive cost!
The dog is covered like a snowman,
While my shoes are a sticky jam.

I rolled out shapes, some looked like blobs,
While icing explosions drew hilarious sobs.
The taste test came, oh what a thrill,
One bite led to a sugar spill!

These moments freeze, a time so sweet,
With every laugh, the heart skips a beat.
So raise your mug, let's toast today,
For sugar-spiced dreams never fade away!

Frosted Euphoria

The frosted windows hide a charm,
While cookies strut, oh what a farm!
The colors gleam, a sight to see,
A frosting party — come join me!

Marshmallow clouds on every treat,
And candy canes that dance on their feet.
The giggling elves are working fast,
Turning flour to magic, and laughter lasts.

Sprinkling joy with careless ease,
The kitchen smells of purest tease.
Cocoa rivers start to flow,
While ginger men put on a show.

Sugar highs and candy dreams,
Fill the room with lively schemes.
So grab a piece, don't hesitate,
In frosted euphoria, we celebrate!

A Slice of Holiday Magic

In the kitchen, chaos reigns,
Flour flying like soft snowflakes,
Ginger men dance with silly grins,
As I trip on my silly mistakes.

Sprinkle sugar, not on my nose!
I'm a chef, but who'd really guess?
My apron's a canvas of dough,
My hair? A masterpiece of mess!

The oven hums a merry tune,
While I giggle at the hot don'ts,
Cookies wink with chocolate chips,
They know my baking never haunts!

Oh, holiday magic fills the air,
With each bite, my worries fade.
Laughter rings like jingle bells,
In our kitchen—the grand parade!

Aroma of Nostalgic Delights

A whiff of spice and I am there,
In Grandma's kitchen, all aglow,
Stirring pots of dreams and whipped cream,
Even the cat joins in the show.

Doughnuts rolling off the floor,
Awkward flips and messy hands,
Why do we always lose the dough?
Ah, the magic, my heart expands!

Nuts and sprinkles splash like confetti,
While I juggle with holiday cheer.
Who needs gifts when you have flour?
Just don't ask me to reappear!

Dancing through the kitchen, oh dear!
Sticky fingers and silly grins,
Baking joy fills every room,
Let the real festivities begin!

Cinnamon Dreams in Winter's Embrace

Scent of cinnamon lingers sweet,
As I twirl, pretending to bake,
My spatula's a magic wand,
A dancing partner, make no mistake!

Oven's like a warm bear hug,
Cozy sweaters? More like vests,
Pies puff up like little balloons,
They giggle while I wear my jest!

Sweaty brows and half a grin,
Too much nutmeg? Did I sigh?
Each bite is like a cozy hug,
Or a sneeze that makes you ask, "Why?"

Dreams of sugar, flour, and fun,
Kisses sprinkled everywhere,
In this icy winter wonderland,
Laughter flies high on the sweet air!

Crumbs of Joy in Air

Crumbs are flying like little stars,
Don't ask how they got on the wall,
Gingerbread men run in delight,
Shouting, "Catch us, if you can!" with a call.

Laughter bubbles like milk on the stove,
While frosting slips and slides,
I paint my masterpiece of joy,
With a side of giggles, oh, what a ride!

My helper's a fuzzy little pup,
Who thinks the floor is his buffet,
He steals a bite; oh what a sight!
The laughter here, it makes my day!

When the holiday lights start to glow,
And cookies come in every shape,
The cheery crumbs drift through the air,
Telling tales of joy and escape!

A Dance of Flavors

In a kitchen where laughter flows,
Spices twirl in their little toes.
Sugar plumps up with glee,
While flour flirts with the cheeky tea.

Nutmeg spins, it's quite a sight,
Cinnamon winks, oh what delight!
Clove does a jig, the butter sighs,
As frosting sneaks in, with sugary lies.

Whiskers whisked, a charming mess,
Eggs get cracked, a frothy dress.
Cooking up chaos, flour in the air,
Laughter erupts everywhere!

But soon our treat takes center stage,
Candied joy to all engage.
With a giggle and a crunchy bite,
We're dancing now, pure delight!

Frosting Kisses

Frosting winks like it's in a play,
Whipping cream on parade today.
Minty whispers, sweet dreams unfold,
As sprinkles shimmer like tales of old.

Icing grins, confetti'd cheer,
Jelly beans hide, oh dear, oh dear!
Cupcakes giggle, "Take a bite!"
Brownies chuckle, "We're out of sight!"

Candies tangle in a sugary hug,
Chocolate truffles, all snug as a bug.
Sugar plops and jelly hops,
Lollipops dance till the flavor stops.

With every taste, a bit of bliss,
In every nibble, a frosted kiss.
So come and savor this sweet affair,
In frosting dreams, there's joy to share!

Tales from the Bakery

In the corner, a loaf begins to chat,
'Did you hear about the cupcake spat?'
With muffins giggling from the crate,
Scones retell the tale of fate.

Cookies clamor with chocolate chips,
Whiskers whisking at their lips.
Pies slyly plot to steal the show,
As bakers peek at the doughy glow.

Baker's hats are way too tall,
Rolling pins join in the brawl.
The oven calls out, "Time for fun!"
As pastries dance and giggles run.

Every batch, a story rich,
Laughter baked in, no need for a switch.
So heed the tales of this savory band,
In our bakery world, humor's always planned!

Hearth, Home, and Spice

The hearth is warm, a cozy place,
Where spices joke and doughs embrace.
Butter slides in with a cheeky smirk,
As ginger whispers, "Let's go berserk!"

Nutty pecans join the dance,
While cakes are caught in a fragrant trance.
With every stir, the giggles rise,
As sugar sprinkles the starry skies.

Psysically speaking, it's quite the sight,
Marzipan prances in the moonlight.
With a pinch of salt and a sprinkle of cheer,
They gather around as flavors appear.

So grab a slice, don't be shy,
In this warm hearth, flavors fly.
With laughter and spice, our hearts are full,
In our sugary world, life's never dull!

Sweetness in the Air

Whiffs of sugar dance and play,
Elves in aprons, hip-hip-hooray!
Gingersnap goodies stacked so high,
Even the cat can't help but sigh.

Baking blunders, flour fights,
Mom's recipe for all the nights.
Sprinkles fly like tiny stars,
Sweet chaos in our tasty jars.

A rolling pin? A gleeful mess,
Sweet scents leave us in distress.
The oven's beeping, cookies pop,
Laughter echoes, can't quite stop!

With each bite, a giggle born,
Sugar dreams, oh how they're worn.
Merry moments dipped in cream,
Baking joy, the sweetest dream!

Memories in a Mixing Bowl

In a bowl the memories churn,
Whisking up as lessons learn.
A dash of spice and a pinch of fun,
Silly sounds 'til the day is done.

Eggs are cracking, laughter lies,
Flour dust clouds, surprise!
Sticky fingers like glue on hands,
Making treats from our wild plans.

The timer tinks, the heat ignites,
Gingerbread shapes in silly sights.
Mom's always shouting, 'Don't eat that!'
But who can resist a frosted hat?

Each bite tells a story true,
Of fun adventures we once knew.
The mixing bowl, a treasure chest,
In every nibble, we are blessed!

Christmas Spice Ballad

Jingle bells ring, spices sing,
Baking treats is a goofy thing.
Rolling dough makes giggles soar,
Messy kitchen? We want more!

A sprinkle here, a frosting spree,
Gingerbread houses, oh what glee!
Snoopy snores as treats take flight,
In the oven, a fragrant sight.

Holiday cheer in every bite,
Cookies glow with pure delight.
Crumbly edges, hugs all 'round,
In this bliss, our joy is found.

Laughter echoes, sweets unite,
A funny dance, holding tight.
As we feast through the cold, long night,
Every treat feels pure and bright!

Crisp Edges, Soft Hearts

Crisp edges call with warmth to share,
Soft hearts melt in the sweetened air.
Gingerbread men with icing smiles,
Dancing around for a hundred miles.

Giggles echo as we devour,
Each little bite is a party hour.
Frosted tips and little hats,
Who knew dough could wear such spats?

Sticky hands and woolly socks,
Who needs toys when there are frocks?
Baking battles, oh what fun,
Each cookie fight is hard-won.

From the oven, a smell divine,
Each crumb recalls a joyful time.
With every batch, our hearts will soar,
For in our kitchen, there's always more!

Sugar Sprinkled Moments

In the kitchen, chaos reigns,
Flour on faces, no one gains.
Spoons are flying, eggs take flight,
Mom laughs hard, what a sight!

Sugar plums dance in our heads,
Baking battles, rolling beds.
Ginger men with silly grins,
Lose their arms, yet still, we win!

Festive Whiffs of Warmth

Oven's humming, timers beep,
Cookies pop, we can't help leap.
Whiffs of spice fill the air,
Gingerbread man—in midair!

Frosting's like a snowstorm blast,
Fingers sticky—it's a blast!
Munching treats, with giggles loud,
We declare ourselves so proud!

Snippets from the Cookie Jar

Peeking in, what do I see?
Starlit dreams of cookies, whee!
Chocolates wink, sprinkles shout,
Who could ever turn them out?

Potato chips or might it be,
My last ginger snack in spree?
In the jar, a heart's delight,
Taking bites 'til the moonlight!

Ginger Dreams on a Frosted Night

Frosted stars twinkle and smile,
Ginger men dance, just for a while.
Snowball fights with sugar dust,
Against the walls, we laugh, we trust.

Royal icing sighs and gleams,
In our hearts, the sweetest dreams.
Baking joy on winter's eve,
Every crumb makes us believe!

Gingered Whispers on the Wind

In a kitchen full of cheer,
Ginger giggles, oh so near.
Cookies dance in flour clouds,
Sugar rush with laughter loud.

Sprinkled smiles and doughy grins,
Ginger men with floppy fins.
They prance upon the countertop,
As sugar fairies spin and hop.

Whispers of spice in the air,
Whirling round without a care.
Laughter simmering like hot tea,
Oh, what fun this joy can be!

When the oven warms the heart,
Chocolate chips and silly art.
With each bite, we can't resist,
A happy dance, we all persist!

Frosted Wishes and Cozy Kisses

With frosting whirls and candy canes,
Giggles echo, joy remains.
Sweetest wishes all around,
In this warmth, pure love is found.

Cookies dressed in jolly hats,
Squeaky corners, playful chats.
Sprinkled dreams on every side,
Cozy thrills we won't abide.

Sugar plums and nutmeg cheer,
Ginger grams bring loved ones near.
Sipping cocoa, we all share,
Funny tales of holiday flair.

Hugs wrapped up like candy treats,
Sharing smiles, it's all so sweet.
With each bite, the laughter flows,
Creating joy where friendship glows.

A Symphony of Sugary Spice

In the bowl, a jolly mix,
Dancing rhythms, silly tricks.
Melodies of sugar rise,
Creating giggles, sweet surprise.

Baking tunes and whisks that sway,
Frosting serenades on display.
Flavors trumpeting a cheer,
Bouncing laughter, spreading here.

Oven's warmth, a cozy hum,
Doughy tunes that make me strum.
Spices whispered, notes collide,
Funny flavors, side by side.

When the cookies come alive,
Jolly vibes, the best to thrive.
Join the dance, the giggles grow,
In this symphony, let's go slow.

Memories Carved in Cookie Molds

In the shapes of merry cheer,
Cookies carved, a smile near.
With every bite, a tale unfolds,
Funny stories, pure as gold.

Spices mingling, friends unite,
Ginger snaps on a snowy night.
In laughter's glow, we find our way,
Making memories, come what may.

Chocolates melt and giggles swirl,
Sprinkles twinkling, watch them twirl.
Each cookie holds a secret song,
A memory where we belong.

With a pinch of spice and cheer,
Every moment feels so dear.
So grab a plate, let's have a feast,
In these delights, we're all released!

Hearthside Cheery Whirls

In the kitchen, laughter brews,
Dough sticks to shoes and gooey glues.
With flour fights that sparkle and fly,
We giggle as we watch the batches lie.

Spices giggle, they dance and swirl,
Belly laughs as they give a twirl.
Mamma's secret, she swears it's true,
Makes all the cookies sing, "Woo-hoo!"

The oven hums a merry tune,
While we juggle dough, we dance like loons.
Sticky fingers reach for snacks,
As giggles escape through our silly cracks.

With each bite, the world turns bright,
Sweet giggles echo in the night.
Who knew that baking could be such fun?
We'll munch and chomp until we're done!

Golden Brown Dreams

Once upon a time, in a pan so wide,
Gingerbread men took a slippery slide.
They shouted, "Catch us if you dare!"
But left sweet footprints everywhere.

With candy eyes and icing hats,
They pranced around like silly brats.
One fell flat right on his face,
"Oops," he said, "I'll win this race!"

Baking time is a wobbly show,
When flour flies like powdered snow.
A pinch of spice, a dash of fun,
Our golden dreams are never done!

As we munch on legless treats,
We laugh at all our funny feats.
Who knew cookies could bring such cheer?
Let's bake ten more, and drink some beer!

Essence of Yuletide Creations

With jingles ringing, dough is mixed,
Ginger hugs the bowl, so fixed.
A sprinkle here and a dash of that,
The batter's grown quite chitchat!

Rolling pins dance like they're alive,
"Make me thin!" the dough screams, "Thrive!"
Cut into shapes, oh what a scene,
Star, hearts, and one big spleen!

In the bake-off, we spin and lurch,
It's mayhem turned into a search.
Out come cookies, golden brown,
The funniest sight in all the town!

Now the platter's full, oh what a hoot,
As we gobble them up, who knew?
With each giggle, a crumb does fly,
Sweet origins of a pie in the sky!

Flavors of a Cozy Hearth

Tiny sprinkles await their fate,
As gingerbread men spin and skate.
Belly laughs bounce off the wall,
In this cozy nook, we have a ball!

With every mix, a new surprise,
Cookie disasters materialize.
One cookie's head is stuck on the floor,
"Hey! Someone, pass me a dough-filled score!"

Baking isn't just for the faint,
It's a circus, wild and quaint.
Each bite tells a story so sweet,
As laughter dances on sugar beats.

So gather 'round for a munchy feast,
Where silly antics never cease.
With memories made of spice and cheer,
These silly treats we hold so dear!

Crumbs of Nostalgia

In the oven, a dance begins,
The batter jiggles, joy wins.
Sneaking tastes before it's baked,
A kitchen full of mischief, unshaken.

Cookie dough on fingers stuck,
A cheeky grin, oh what luck!
Mom's laughter fills the space,
Flour fights make a creamy face.

When the timer dings its tune,
We gobble fast, like hungry raccoons.
Crumbs on noses, sugar sprinkles,
Who knew baking could cause such crinkles?

A dash of chaos, a spoon of delight,
Sugar highs that last till night.
Replaying the antics, loud and bright,
Those sweet little moments feel just right.

Ginger's Cozy Whisper

A ginger snap winks at me,
Oh, you cheeky little spree!
Crunch it once and then again,
Laughing crumbs on my chin, my friend.

A sneaky nibble, another test,
Mom sees, puts my will to the test.
With every bite, giggles arise,
How can I help but devise?

A pinch of spice, a sugar twirl,
In a world that's full of swirl.
Pillows of flavor, a cozy dream,
With each bite, I burst at the seam.

Laughter spirals with warmth all around,
In dessert's circle, we are spellbound.
Ginger's magic, oh what a sight,
Fun in flavors, pure delight!

Spiced Revelations

What's that smell? Oh, I confess,
It's a joyful, spicy mess!
With giggles peeking from every corner,
The cookie sheet pulls a new performer.

An apron on like a superhero's cape,
With swirls of frosting, there's no escape.
Gingerbread men march in a row,
Each crafted with love, oh what a show!

Ready for battles, but oh dear me,
One took a tumble, now it's fleeing free!
A crumbling smile, arms in retreat,
Ginger's warmth wraps me in sweet defeat.

Silly sprinkles dance on my nose,
While my laughter spills, who knows how it goes?
In a world where cookies never quit,
Each bite's a giggle, just a perfect fit!

Aromas of Childhood

In the kitchen, chaos unfolds,
A symphony of stories told.
Whisking gently like a joyful breeze,
Time to bake, oh please, oh please!

Giggles bubble, sugar flies,
A sprinkle here and a dash that sighs.
Taste-testing each frosted delight,
Until I'm dizzy by the first bite.

With ginger dances and laughter bakes,
Every mistake is a giggle that wakes.
In playful flops and candied charms,
Memories hug me in warm, sweet arms.

From rolling pins to sugar swirls,
Magic happens, laughter curls.
Those cozy scents where memories spread,
Are the hidden treasures in my heart's bread.

Memories Meringue

In a kitchen bustling loud,
Flour is flying, oh so proud.
Baking mishaps make us grin,
Eggshells dance while cakes begin.

Sugar sprinkles in the air,
Mixing chaos with a flair.
Batter flying—what a sight!
Who knew baking could be a fright?

Whipped cream clouds on faces bold,
Sticky fingers, stories told.
Giggles echo, laughter spills,
Kitchen magic? Just our skills!

Flavors swirl and pastries soar,
Creating joy, we want more.
Meringues bounce and cookies laugh,
In this recipe for fun, we craft!

Sugared Trails of Happiness

Oh, the trails of sweetness shine,
Candy colors, all divine.
Marshmallow mountains, chocolate streams,
Each step feels just like a dream.

Gumdrops glisten, jellies sway,
A path of joy, come what may.
Cake pops dance, sprinkles twirl,
In this sugary wonder world.

Lollipops sing, candy canes cheer,
Tickling noses, spreading cheer.
Giggling hosts at every turn,
For each sweet bite, our hearts yearn.

Gingerbread houses with gumdrop roofs,
Silly smiles and playful goofs.
Come join us on this jolly ride,
Where happiness can't hide!

Hearth-Cooked Love Stories

Gather 'round the hearth so bright,
Pies and laughter fill the night.
Grandma's tales with warming sighs,
Currants giggle, cinnamon flies.

Ovens bubbling, aromas swirl,
You know it's time to give a twirl.
Flour-covered socks and shoes,
Every bite feels like good news.

Chocolate chips like tiny stars,
Come together, healing scars.
We bake our dreams in fluffy crusts,
In kitchen chaos, love we trust.

Each recipe's a secret script,
With smudges of joy, we've equipped.
Hearth-cooked tales, sweet and tender,
Cooked with humor, love to render!

A Journey of Vanilla Dreams

Join us on this creamy quest,
Where clouds of vanilla are the best.
A sprinkle here, a dash of that,
Each whimsy treat, a playful spat.

Marzipan roads, a sugar scene,
Past caramel rivers, we're so keen.
Cupcake castles, frosting mayors,
Bouncing around in our sweet prayers.

In this land, we leap and bound,
With custard cream, joy is found.
Whipped delights on our plate,
Gallivanting, let's celebrate!

Through cookie forests, laughter blooms,
Every step beyond gloom.
In the heart of this sugary dream,
Funny flavors reign supreme!

Holiday's Warmest Embrace

In the oven, a dance begins,
Sugar and spice, let the chaos spin.
Baking fails, oh what a sight,
Unruly cookies take flight!

Flour fights with every whisk,
Frosting clumps, a sweet redisk.
Ginger men, they laugh and play,
Who knew baking turned out this way?

Mischief hides in each warm bite,
Merry moments, pure delight.
Sugar rush and giggles shared,
Who knew we'd be mildly scared?

Laughter echoes, a whirlwind cheer,
With each mess, we hold more dear.
Sweetness wraps the laughter tight,
In every cookie's silly flight.

Nostalgic Snippets of Frosting Dreams

Grandma's apron, flour dusted,
In the kitchen, we're always busted.
Frosting fights paint our faces,
With gingerbread, we found our places.

Building houses, but they sink,
Oh no, look, there goes the clink!
Candy roofs, they wobble, sway,
Let's just eat them anyway!

Nostalgic smells in the air,
Can't resist that frosted dare.
Baking with giggles and spills,
Tasting joy, oh what a thrill!

As cookies smile and winks play,
We'll eat our art, come what may.
Frosted memories, bold and sweet,
What a joy, this tasty feat!

Chewy Joys and Creamy Clouds

Mixing sugar, a swirl so bright,
Joy sparks in every bite.
Chewy treats, soft as a dream,
Laughter flows like a sweet cream.

Baking bits of silly charms,
Frosting blobs with hopeful arms.
Kitchen chaos in every hue,
Cookies giggle, we join too!

With sprinkles flying like confetti,
Oh, what fun when things get messy!
A lopsided stack, but who will mind?
Each bite is joy, uniquely designed.

As we munch on giddy dreams,
Life's sweeter, or so it seems.
With giggles wrapped in doughy shrouds,
We feast in chewy, creamy clouds.

Gingered Threads of a Season's Quilt

Gather 'round, let's weave this tale,
With spicy laughs on a sugary trail.
A quilt of cookies, oh what a sight,
Each piece tells stories all through the night.

Pinch of ginger, dash of giggle,
Frosting rivers make us wiggle.
Baking disasters make us cheer,
Flavors of warmth, we hold them dear.

Granny's spice, a sprinkle of love,
Dancing ginger, it fits like a glove.
Crafted with laughter, stitched with care,
Each cookie's story fills the air.

So raise a glass to the mess we make,
In every crumb, there's joy to take.
Gingered threads twined through our feast,\nIn every bite,
we're never least.

Whirls of Festive Spice

In a kitchen where chaos reigns,
Flour flies like snow in playful gains.
A doughy dragon begins to rise,
With candy eyes and a sugar disguise.

Mixers whirl like a dance of glee,
While a rolling pin joins the jamboree.
Ginger snaps jump and try to flee,
As sprinkles rain down like confetti spree.

Piping bags wiggle in a colorful show,
As frosting starts to twirl and glow.
The taste buds cheer, 'Oh what a treat!'
In this whimsical world, life's hard to beat.

When friends arrive, with cookies in hand,
We laugh and munch, it's truly grand.
Each bite's a giggle, a sugary jest,
In this season of spice, we're truly blessed!

Winter's Edible Embrace

In a frosty world where flavors play,
We bake with joy and eat all day.
Our oven's a furnace, and can't you see?
Even the spatula dances with glee!

A pinch of this and a sprinkle that,
Our cat's on the counter, what's with the spat?
He eyes the dough with a devious grin,
Trying to sneak a nibble or win.

Ginger men prance with a sugary twist,
If they could run, they'd surely enlist.
Chasing each other around on the plate,
Laughing at danger; oh, isn't it great?

As carols play softly, we munch and cheer,
Each doughy delight brings good cheer near.
With icing smiles, we share the tale,
Of baking adventures that never fail!

Whisked Away in Spice

Whirls of brown sugar and nutmeg's song,
Blend in a bowl, it can't be wrong.
A spoon starts to dance with a cheerfully clatter,
As crumbs go flying, what's the matter?

We form little houses; they lean to one side,
A gingerbread couple takes a wild ride.
Decorations tumble, oh what a mess,
But oh, how we love this sugary stress!

Frosting rivers flow, and candy trees sprout,
As gumdrops gather for a merry rout.
Each bite's a giggle, each taste a delight,
In this frosted land, we dance through the night!

As laughter echoes, the cookies upstage,
They wink and they nod, 'It's all the rage!'
With each little nibble, a chuckle breaks free,
In this warm kitchen, we're as happy as can be.

Whispers of a Bakery's Heart

In the heart of the bakery, aromas collide,
Where laughter and giggles are hard to hide.
A doughy delight with a sprinkle of fun,
Brings joy to our hearts, like a race just begun.

The oven hums soft, a lullaby sweet,
While cinnamon swirl takes a twirling seat.
It whispers of warmth, of joy to impart,
Each morsel a hug, a cozy warm heart.

The gingerbreads form a committee today,
Debating their frosting, oh what do they say?
'With sparkles and colors, we'll steal the show!'
Routed only by the aromas they grow.

In the midst of the chaos, our friends gather near,
Decked out in aprons, we spread lots of cheer.
With each tasty bite of our holiday fare,
We laugh through the season, none can compare!

Spiced Reflections of Laughter

In a kitchen, chaos reigns,
Flour flies like snow on planes.
Cookies dance on the counter's edge,
Sugar's laughter is a playful pledge.

Ginger giggles, spice takes flight,
Caught in the whisk, oh what a sight!
Baking fails have us in stitches,
Our dough's more like a bowl of glitches.

The oven's warmth, a crafty thief,
Steals our time, but brings us relief.
Gingerbread men with missing feet,
Are the stars of our baking feat!

So raise your spatula, sing aloud,
In this kitchen, we're a silly crowd.
With every laugh, our hearts are fed,
Baked delights and joy are wed.

A Mosaic of Baked Love

Piping frosting in a wild spree,
Ribbons tangled like a mystery.
Cookies shaped like a clumsy cat,
What's next? A cake shaped like a hat!

Sugar sprinkles rain from above,
Creating art we surely love.
Ginger flakes in the batter swirl,
When it's done, we give it a twirl!

Our baking fails, a tapestry bright,
Each burnt edge, a humorous sight.
And with each bite of our sweet disaster,
We laugh and eat, the fun comes faster!

So gather 'round for a ginger snort,
A mosaic of treats, of fun we report.
With laughter and crumbs on the floor,
Our love's a recipe we can't ignore.

Comfort's Gingered Essence

In the bowl, a little chaos thrives,
Mixing giggles, where mischief jives.
Ginger hugs the butter tight,
As we whisk dreams late into the night.

Oh, the mess! A floury mound,
Sprinkled laughter all around.
The cookies rise with smiles so wide,
As we munch on the gingered pride.

Chocolate chips run for their lives,
As we create our cookie archives.
With icing that doesn't quite make the cut,
We laugh so hard, our sides will jut!

Comfort comes, from oven so warm,
In bursts of laughter, we find our charm.
Gingerbread joys, in every bite,
Sprinkled with humor, oh what a sight!

Whirling Ginger Stars

In a dance of flour, we twirl and spin,
Baking ginger gems with a cheeky grin.
Each star a wonder, a little delight,
But sometimes they just take flight!

Dough on the ceiling, oh what a climb,
Baked abandon at the speed of rhyme.
Mishaps burst in a sugar plume,
While ginger snap snickers fill the room.

Our taste tests end up in comedy,
Savoring joy in absurdity.
Baking's a circus, join the fun,
Taste buds giggling, second to none!

So twinkling stars in a crunchy mess,
We laugh at our gingered success.
With every crumb, our spirits cheer,
Whirling through baking, we hold dear.

Woodland Fairies and Ginger Secrets

In the woods where fairies dance,
They whisper secrets, take a chance.
With tiny giggles, they all conspire,
Baking treats that never tire.

A sprinkle here, a pinch of joy,
Mischief brewed in every ploy.
Ginger snaps the bunnies bake,
While cheeky elves just laugh and quake.

With tiny spoons and oversized bowls,
They stir the mix, achieving goals.
A frosted roof on every treat,
Complaints of ants, oh so sweet!

They feast on cookies made of dreams,
While plotting pranks, or so it seems.
In this forest, laughter's bright,
With ginger goodies, day and night.

A Dash of Magic.

A sprinkle of magic in every bite,
A dash of giggles, pure delight.
From cookie wands, the spells arise,
With ginger dust and twinkling eyes.

The oven hums a jolly tune,
While chefs are dancing with a spoon.
Laughter bubbles, cookies bloom,
In the warm, inviting kitchen room.

Silly hats upon their heads,
Gingerbread men in tricky beds.
"Don't eat me!" one cookie cries,
As frosting hides its joyful sighs.

With each soft bite, their antics free,
As ginger snaps take flight, you see.
In every crumb, joy does stick,
A dash of fun, a tasty trick.

Warmth of Spiced Memories

In the hearth, a memory brews,
Whiffs of ginger mixed with blues.
Grandma's laughter fills the space,
With silly faces, oh what grace.

Stirring pots with flair and flair,
"Just one more cookie!" fills the air.
Sugar sprinkles, giggles rare,
In the warmth, all joys declare.

A clumsy elf trips on the floor,
While tasting batches, smells galore.
The dough is binding, laughter too,
With friendly bakes, we start anew.

In spiced cookies, we all unite,
Sharing stories, hearts so light.
Each bite a memory that sings,
Wrapped in warmth, the joy it brings.

Whispers of Sugar and Spice

In the kitchen, whispers play,
From sugar dreams to spice ballet.
Ginger stories swirl around,
With twinkling eyes, they astound.

A spatula's dance, a dash of fun,
Baking's best when it's all done.
Sugar flour flying high,
As cookie tales flutter by.

Mischief's sneaking, elves on cue,
Ginger puffed, oh what a view!
With a giggle and a little shove,
They bake together in pure love.

So gather 'round, sweet friends, arise,
With every laugh, the spirit flies.
In every bite, the joy ignites,
As we feast under starry nights.

Cookies in the Twilight

In the kitchen, chaos reigns,
Flour flies like snowy rains.
A whisk took flight, oh what a sight,
A doughy monster crawls tonight!

Ovens giggle, timers beep,
While kittens plot a cookie creep.
They dance around with frosting dreams,
And plot sweet schemes to bake in teams!

A cookie jar now guards the feast,
But crumbs betray our hunger beast.
With laughter bubbling, we will hit,
The last cookie, every bit!

So gather round, let fun ensue,
For cookie magic's made for you.
In twilight's glow, we reign supreme,
In a sugary, silly, starlit dream!

Whimsy Baked in Sugar Dust

In a world where cookies dance,
Frosting swirls, a cheering chance.
Sugar sprinkles fill the air,
As giggles turn the day to flair.

Ginger folks with tiny hats,
Dance on tables, toss some chats.
With each nibble, laughter bursts,
Their silly antics quench our thirsts!

A pie in the sky begins to float,
Caught in a whimsical, frosting boat.
Laughter rises with each sweet bite,
In a sugar dream, we taste the night!

So grab a spoon, let's stir it right,
In this bakery of pure delight.
The fun we bake, it's never cursed,
For joy is found in what we burst!

Hearth of Happiness

By the hearth, the laughter's bright,
Cookies smile—what a sight!
With chocolate chips, they wink and sway,
Inviting all for a joyful play.

A spatula winks with glee,
As flour fights are fun, you see.
A secret stash! Oh, where's it hid?
Among the laughs, we peek and skid!

Rolling pins are swords of joy,
As each brave chef, a playful boy.
With butter pats and sugar moons,
We create our sweet-tasting tunes!

So gather 'round this happy nest,
In cookie chaos, we are blessed.
With crumbs of giggles, hugs abound,
In this hearth, true joy is found!

Enchanted Bakery Quest

In a land of dough and spoons,
We embark on tasty looney tunes.
Sugar trails lead us on the way,
To cookie castles where fairies play.

A cupcake lion roars with cheer,
While gummy bears provide the beer.
Waffles sing as syrup flows,
In this quest for treats, joy grows!

The journey swirls with pies galore,
Muffins bouncing, we shout for more!
With every step, our laughter rings,
As we seek out those tasty things!

So come along, don your chef hat,
In this enchanted world, we chat.
With sugar dreams and laughter's zest,
In this bakery, we are blessed!

Cookie Tales Under Twinkling Stars

Under the stars, cookies dance with glee,
A sprinkle of laughter, as sweet as can be.
The flour flies high, a storm in the night,
While doughy creatures take off in delight.

With chocolate chip hats and icing galore,
They giggle and jiggle, always wanting more.
A cupcake brigade joins the midnight spree,
Trading frosting for tales of pure jubilee.

A gingerbread house stands tall and proud,
With windows that wink and a frosting crowd.
They host a grand ball on a vanilla cloud,
Kicking up flour, oh, how they're loud!

As the sun peeks in, the fun starts to wane,
But the memories linger, like a sugar cane.
With crumbs on their feet, they'll march on their way,
Till the next twinkling night, where they frolic and play.

Joy in a Morsel

A cookie's first bite brings giggles so bright,
With sprinkles that twinkle, a candy delight.
Each crumble of happiness, laughter in chunks,
A morsel of joy, as silliness thunks.

In ovens they dream, in their sugary coats,
Doughy adventurers, on sweet little boats.
They sail through the air, on frosting-made tides,
While pies in the windows just giggle and hide.

A munch and a crunch, a symphony plays,
Of giggles and snorts in the cookie parade.
With marshmallow hats, they sway side to side,
As the flavors unite in a frolicsome ride.

But soon comes the time to say a fond cheer,
To crumbs and sweet moments, we hold ever dear.
In a dance of delights, they bid us goodbye,
Till the next batch of joy makes us laugh 'til we cry.

Warm Spice Chronicles

In the heart of the kitchen, spices unite,
With ginger and nutmeg, oh what a sight!
The cinnamon whirlwinds bring giggling flair,
As the dough starts to shimmer, a flavorful dare.

Each sprinkle of sugar, a fairy tale spun,
With buttered-up dreams, oh, isn't this fun?
They twirl on the counter, with spoons as their crew,
Banishing boredom with a sugary stew.

An army of cupcakes, with frosting so bright,
Regale us with tales of their sweet, silly night.
A cookie's mischief leads to marshmallow fights,
And soon, laughter erupts, lighting up all the sights.

As we bake up the magic, let giggles arise,
With flavors that tickle and twinkle the eyes.
For every warm cookie, a moment we cheer,
In the chronicles born from the warmth of the year.

Wandering Through a Sugary Dream

In a dream made of sugar, I float and I glide,
Past rivers of chocolate, where giggles abide.
Marshmallow clouds drift with a sugary breeze,
While candy canes sway, bringing sweet memories.

A gingerbread man chuckles, he's quick on his feet,
He challenges cupcakes, oh, what a sweet feat!
They race through the fields of peppermint lanes,
In a whirlwind of laughter, they dodge all the gains.

Donut-shaped suns rise, with sprinkles for rays,
As laughter echoes through comical days.
The frosting that twirls makes the moments so bright,
Wandering, we whirl in this magical night.

But the dawn is now peeking, the dream starts to fade,
With crumbs of sweet joy in the world that we made.
So hold on to the giggles, the laughter, the gleam,
And cherish each morsel from our sugary dream.

Airborne Ginger Joys

In the oven, a dance begins,
Ginger leaps with floury grins,
Sugary thrills from the brown delight,
Cookies soaring, oh what a sight!

Baking trays on a wild ride,
Laughter mixes with spice and pride,
Frosting giggles as sprinkles jump,
In the sugar rush, we all thump!

Rolling pins, they glide and spin,
While cheeky sprats are sneaking in,
Chasing crumbs, all giddy and spry,
With every bite, oh my, oh my!

A whiff drifts out to tickle your nose,
As laughter frolics, and giggles rose,
Even the cats join in the fun,
With mischievous paws, they're never done!

Whisking Through Time

Time flies in a whirlwind of dough,
Whisks are dancing, oh look at them go,
Grandma's secrets all mixed with cheer,
Making memories, year after year.

Each swirl of spice brings forth a laugh,
As we measure out joy by the half,
Eggs are cracking with giggly glee,
How sweet the chaos, just wait and see!

A whisking wizard in floury disguise,
Sprinkling laughter that never denies,
In the kitchen, friendships start to bloom,
With every stir, there's more room for zoom!

As the timer pings, we dance with glee,
Hands sticky sweet, not a single plea,
Bite into heaven, what do we stumble?
A giggly trip through a doughy jumble!

Morsels of Celebration

Gather 'round for a bite that sings,
Morsels sprinkled with magical things,
Each crumb's a party, a giggle club,
With laughter rising, not a single grub.

Bite-sized chit-chats and cheeky smiles,
A parade of treats across the miles,
Nibbles that tickle and blush your cheeks,
With every crunch, our happiness peaks!

Frosting fights in the colorful fray,
Piping bags come out to join the play,
Sugar battles turn into sweet cheers,
Each crumb holds the laughter of years.

Sing a song with a cookie in hand,
As friends gather round, all perfectly planned,
The celebration kicks up like the loudest game,
In every morsel, the joy stays the same!

Caramelized Echoes of Uplift

A sprinkle of joy, a dash of fate,
Caramel whispers: "Don't hesitate!"
Golden moments in candy embrace,
A sticky giggle, a celebratory race.

Warmth fills the air as they bubble and brew,
Echoes of laughter, all shiny and new,
Batches of sweetness causing commotion,
Each spoony stir ignites the emotion.

Come one, come all, let's feast and play,
Ginger snaps make troubles float away,
In this mushy bliss, we can't stay still,
With every bite, more sugar to spill!

Frolic through flavors, a dance we'll create,
Even the burnt ones, we'll celebrate,
Let's hoot and holler at each little bite,
In this sweet chaos, everything feels right!

Sweetened Hearth Tales

In the kitchen, a happy dance,
Flour flies in a whirlwind prance.
Ginger's winks and sugar's glee,
Bringing laughter to you and me.

Baking giggles, oh what a sight,
Cookies laughing, full of delight.
Sprinkles tumble, they have a fling,
Silly shapes, oh, what fun they bring!

Rolling pins spinning like tops,
Dough in knots, oh, never stops.
"Is that a cookie or a pancake?"
A moment to pause, a bellyache!

And when they're done, we'll make a fuss,
Eating treats without a rush.
With every bite, the joy combines,
Sweet tales shared through sugary signs.

Cookie Crumbs of Contentment

Little hands with doughy pride,
Mixing chaos, oh what a ride!
Chocolate chips hide and seek,
Sugary smiles and giggles peak.

Pans are clanging, oh such a sound,
Gingerbread men dancing around.
One fell down, we all burst out,
Who knew cookies could make us shout?

A sprinkle fight breaks out in glee,
Colorful clouds as bright as can be.
"Decorate me," the doughnuts plead,
"Oh, add some more, just one more bead!"

When all is done and flavors blend,
We gather 'round with every friend.
Sharing crumbs of sweet delight,
Contentment served, oh what a night!

Decorating the Hearth with Cheer

On the hearth, a colorful riot,
Cookies come alive, oh, try it!
With icing floods, they jump and slide,
Dancing rainbow sprinkles wide.

Baking blunders, who made that face?
A cookie monster in the race!
Who could know dough could be so bold,
With stories baked and secrets told?

Candy canes in a pickle jar,
Gingerbread folks wishing on a star.
Frosting rivers, a sticky spree,
Decorating with wild jubilee!

When the hearth is filled with cheer,
Laughter echoes, bringing near.
More sprinkles here, oh, what a sight,
Everyone grins at this pure delight!

A Festive Batterscape

In the oven, a batter blooms,
Whisking up giggles and fluffy looms.
Silly faces, doughy grins,
Guess who'll win? Oh, let's begin!

Rolling the dough with joyful flair,
Gingerbread men everywhere!
Some are tall, some could flop,
Who knew cookies could make us hop?

"Oops, that's not a star, it's a blob!"
Laughter shared, each joyful bob.
Sprinkled laughter fills the air,
A fun-filled kitchen, aromas rare.

When the day comes to an end,
We toast our cookies, each one a friend.
In a batterscape of taste and cheer,
Sweet memories linger throughout the year!

Milton Keynes UK
Ingram Content Group UK Ltd.
UKHW020735301124
451807UK00019B/795